Greatest Goofiest Jokes

Greatest Goofiest Jokes

By Terry Pierce

Illustrated by Buck Jones

STERLING PUBLISHING CO., INC.
New York

Library of Congress Cataloging-in-Publication Data

Pierce, Terry.
  Greatest goofiest jokes / Terry Pierce.
    p. cm.
  Includes index.
  ISBN 1-4027-0769-X
    1. Wit and humor, Juvenile. [1. Jokes. 2. Riddles.] I. Title.
PN6166.P56 2004
818'.602--dc22

                         2003024867

10 9 8 7 6 5 4 3 2 1

Published by Sterling Publishing Co., Inc.
387 Park Avenue South, New York, NY 10016
© 2004 by Terry Pierce
Distributed in Canada by Sterling Publishing
C/o Canadian Manda Group, One Atlantic Avenue, Suite 105
Toronto, Ontario, Canada M6K 3E7
Distributed in Great Britain and Europe by Chris Lloyd at Orca Book
Services, Stanley House, Fleets Lane, Poole BH15 3AJ, England
Distributed in Australia by Capricorn Link (Australia) Pty. Ltd.
P.O. Box 704, Windsor, NSW 2756, Australia

Printed in China

Sterling ISBN 1-4027-0769-X

Contents

1. **A**nimal **A**ntics

What do birds do for entertainment?
  They tell yolks.

Where do crows buy juice drinks?
  At the crowbar.

Where do crows learn to fly?
  At caw-llege.

What goes after a cockatoo?
  A cockathree.

What's the best thing to do for a bluebird?
  Cheer it up.

Why was Mother Owl upset with Junior Owl?
  Because he didn't give a hoot about doing his homework.

How do you stop a crow from cawing?
  Take away its phone.

Why did the customer refuse to pay the stork?
Its bill was too high.

How would you describe cheerful waterfowl?
Happy-go-ducky.

Why was the duck so grouchy?
It was always in a fowl mood.

How do you fix a broken duck?
With duck-tape.

What would you call a royal bird's adopted dog?
A regal eagle's legal beagle.

What kind of dogs play in a band?
Rocker spaniels.

What do you call an amazing little dog?
A Chi-wow-wow.

Why was the dog twitching so much?
It had a tic.

FIDO: I can't go to dog obedience school tonight.
SPOT: Why not?
FIDO: My master ate my homework.

Why are sheep bad dog-trainers?
Because ewe can't teach an old dog new tricks.

It's a Dog's Life

What's a dog's favorite dessert?
An ice cream bone.

What's a dog's favorite vegetable?
Collared greens.

What's a dog's favorite rainy day activity?
Jumping in poodles.

What's a dog's favorite book?
Grimm's Hairy Tales.

What's a dog's favorite vacation spot?
The Swiss Yelps.

What's a dog's favorite music group?
The Rolling Bones.

What's a dog's favorite movie snack?
Pupcorn.

Why did the kennel go out of business?
It went to the dogs.

How do dogs talk to each other on the computer?
By flea-mail.

What kind of dog hangs out at a marina?
A docks-hund.

Why is golf a dog's favorite game?
It loves being in the ruff.

Where do cats put their trash?
In the litter box.

Why did the cat eat lemons?
It was a sour puss.

Who was the first cat to come to America?
Christo-fur Colum-puss.

What did the mother cat say when her kittens were all asleep?
"No mews is good mews."

Why don't zebras like to color?
They won't stay between the lions.

Did you hear about the lion-grooming contest in New England?
It was the Maine event.

Why did the lion cross the road?
To get to the other pride.

Why did the rhinoceros blow its horn?
It had a cold.

Why did the elephants go on strike?
They were tired of working for peanuts.

Why did the elephant lay its head on the piano?
It wanted to play by ear.

How do you fit an elephant in a sports car?
   Put the top down.

How do you fit a giraffe in a sports car?
   Cover it with shortening.

What did the giraffe say to the elephant as they
boarded Noah's ark?
   "We're all in the same boat!"

How do you turn an elephant into an insect?
   Take away the "eleph."

Unwritten Books

Eagle Watching by C.M. Soar.

Midnight Howls by Ali Katz.

Life in the Arctic Ocean by I. C. Waters.

Outrunning Lions by Hugo Fast.

Pet Grooming by Harry Dahgs.

Why did the girl swallow a fly?
She had a frog in her throat.

What do you call a couple of clumsy fireflies?
Blunder and lightning.

Where do bees sleep?
In a flowerbed.

Why do spiders live in cornfields?
So they can build cob-webs.

Why couldn't the snake sue the pet store?
It didn't have a leg to stand on.

How quiet is a snake pit?
You can hear a skin drop.

Why are snakes so easy to take care of?
They make a little food go a long way.

How do you clean a sheep?
Give it a baa-th.

Where do you clean a bat?
In the bat-tub.

How do you clean a crow?
Run it through the caw-wash.

Why was the skunk broke?
It was always putting in its two scents worth.

Why was the baby kangaroo so lazy?
It was a pouch potato.

When do wolves howl the most?
On Moon-day.

Which animals are terrific storytellers?
Monkeys, because they have the best tales.

What animal is dull at parties?
A boar.

What is a pig's favorite relative?
Its oinkle.

What would you get if you crossed a mouse and a parrot?
An animal that eats only cheese and crackers.

Why did the pony eat cough drops?
It was a little hoarse.

What animal is a sweetie?
A deer.

Laughing 'Til The Cows Come Home

What do little cows like to read?
Dairy tales.

What is a cow's favorite game?
Dodge bull.

What's a cow's favorite sandwich?
Peanut-udder and jelly.

What's a cow's favorite song?
*Beethoven's
Moo-nlight
Sonata.*

Why was the cow
such a gossiper?
*She told
all she herd.*

Where do chickens leave the coop?
At the eggs-it.

What do you call a rabbit that does dangerous stunts?
A hare-devil.

What kind of sweaters do bald rabbits want?
Mo-hare.

2. Giggles and Snorts

Why do dogs giggle?
Because they're tick-lish!

Why did the photographer take pictures on windy days?
He liked to shoot the breeze.

Where should parents-to-be invest their money?
In the stork market.

DENTIST: Johnny, you're not brushing your teeth very well. Do you know what comes after decay?
JOHNNY: De "L"?

What's the difference between a chicken inspector and a skunk?
One smells fowl and the other is foul-smelling.

What did Mona Lisa say when she was hauled into court?
"I was framed!"

Why was the garbage man feeling so blue?
He was down in the dumps.

How do you fire. . .?

How do you fire woodworkers?
Tell them they're finished.

How do you fire watch repair people?
Tell them their time is up.

How do you fire teachers?
Tell them they're dismissed.

How do you fire authors?
Tell them it's The End.

How do you fire lumberjacks?
Give them the ax.

How do you fire garbage collectors?
Tell them they're canned.

How do you fire gift-wrappers?
Tell them the job is all wrapped up.

What would you get if you crossed a comedian and a frog?

A practical croaker.

What would you get if you crossed a doctor with a really tight pair of shoes?

Someone who heals your pain and pains your heels.

What would you get if you crossed a chiropractor and a detective?

Someone who can crack your back and crack your case at the same time.

How do mystery writers hold up their pants?

With suspensers.

What do farmers use to light their fields at night?
A flarecrow.

Where did people dance in Medieval times?
In knight clubs.

Which city is the joke capital of America?
Omaha-ha, Nebraska.

Which composer do knights like the most?
Moat-zart.

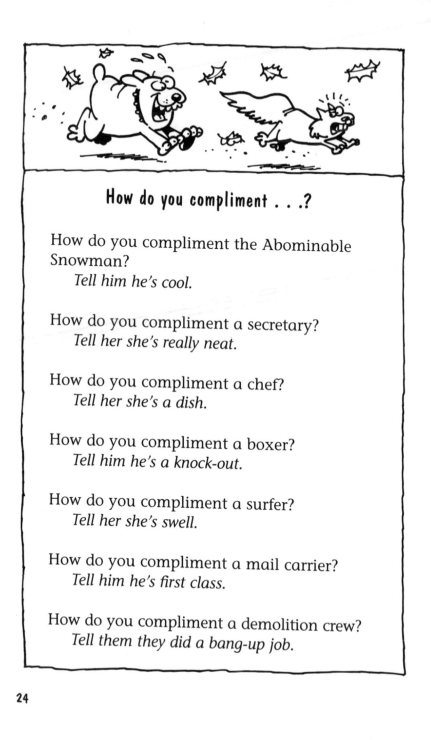

How do you compliment . . .?

How do you compliment the Abominable Snowman?
Tell him he's cool.

How do you compliment a secretary?
Tell her she's really neat.

How do you compliment a chef?
Tell her she's a dish.

How do you compliment a boxer?
Tell him he's a knock-out.

How do you compliment a surfer?
Tell her she's swell.

How do you compliment a mail carrier?
Tell him he's first class.

How do you compliment a demolition crew?
Tell them they did a bang-up job.

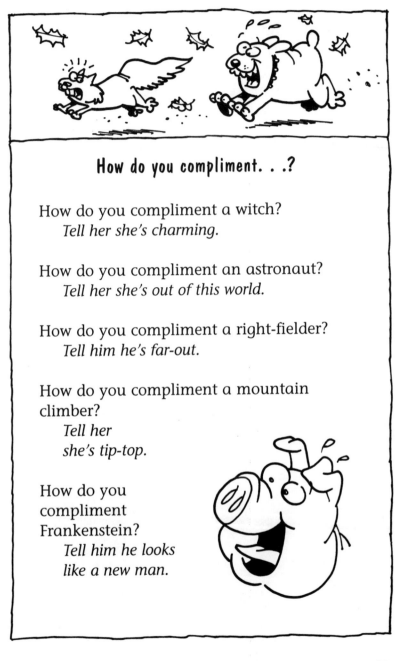

How do you compliment. . .?

How do you compliment a witch?
Tell her she's charming.

How do you compliment an astronaut?
Tell her she's out of this world.

How do you compliment a right-fielder?
Tell him he's far-out.

How do you compliment a mountain climber?
Tell her she's tip-top.

How do you compliment Frankenstein?
Tell him he looks like a new man.

Why are almond growers paid so little?
Because they're good for nuttin'.

Why do pencils make good lawyers?
They always make their points.

What do you call a woman who builds wire fences?
Barb.

How tough is a carpenter?
Tough as nails.

Why did Jerry move his bed to the woods after tossing and turning at home?
So he could sleep like a log.

Who slept in a traffic jam for 100 years?
Beeping Beauty.

3.
Food for Thought

What is a lobster's favorite dessert?
Beaches and cream.

What is a dog's favorite dessert?
Pupcakes.

Why did the boy like pancakes better than cereal?
Pancakes tasted batter.

What do you call a battle in your pantry?
Jar wars.

Why did the girl nibble on her calendar?
She wanted a sundae.

What do sunbathers eat for breakfast?
Toast and eggs sunny-side up.

What does a bald eagle eat for breakfast?
Snake and eggs.

What has lots of dough and rolls?
A baker on skates.

Why was the baker such a bad comedian?
His jokes were all stale.

Why did the actor audition at the bakery?
He only wanted a small role.

What did the baking contest winner say?
"Beauty is in the pie of the beholder."

What did the man say when his bakery was destroyed by an earthquake?
"That's the way the cookie crumbles!"

Knock-knock.
Who's there?
Duncan.
Duncan who?
Duncan cookies in milk is yummy!

Knock-Knock.
Who's there?
Kareem.
Kareem who?
Kareem tastes good in coffee.

Why did the waitress make so much coffee?
It was all in a day's perk.

What does a lizard like to eat with his burger?
  Curly flies.

What do monks eat for dinner?
  Holy chow.

Why did the chips and salsa stop in the road?
  The sign said DIP.

How do you scramble eggs?
g-e-s-g.

What is the best time to cook eggs?
On Fry-days.

How do you make a root beer float?
With a very tiny life jacket.

Why did the boy throw tuna against the wall?
He wanted to see the fishstick.

CECILIA: My Asian cooking class ended early last
night.
LISA: Why?
CECILIA: The teacher woked out.

What do you call a twelve-inch hotdog?
  A frankfooter.

What did the mama lima bean say to the baby lima bean?
  "Have you bean good?"

What did one potato say to the other potato?
  "Keep your eyes peeled."

What's the best way to send a message to a vegetable?
  Pea-mail.

Knock-knock.
Who's there?
Emil.
Emil who?
Emil sounds good right now. I'm hungry.

What did the vegetarian eat for lunch?
Yamburgers and fries.

JACK: Do you know how long fish should be cooked?
JILL: Probably the same amount of time as short fish.

Why did the crook rob the bakery?
He needed the dough.

What's a chiropractor's favorite snack?
Crackers.

Why are seafood restaurants dangerous?
They often have a man eating shark.

How do you clean a chef?
Wash him with soup and water.

What kind of watch should a chef wear?
One that keeps good thyme.

Why were the two watches arguing?
They were ticked off.

What do you call a boy who likes to cook?
Stew.

Why did the garbage man have such a big stomach?
Because everything he ate went to waist.

Knock-Knock.
Who's there?
Abbey.
Abbey who?
Abbey home for dinner.

4. Fishy Funnies

What do fish do for entertainment?
They play cod games.

What is a seal's favorite card game?
Go fish.

What did the fish teacher say to her school?
"Attention, gills and buoys."

Why are fish good comedians?
They're always finny.

Who is the handyman of the sea?
The hammerhead shark.

How do shark parents discipline their children?
They chew them out.

Knock-knock?
Who's there?
Mako sharks.
Mako sharks who?
Mako sharks go away!

Where do sharks sleep?
In a seabed.

What is the saddest sea mammal?
The blue whale.

What do whales eat on their salads?
Alfalfa spouts.

What do whales use to turn their pancakes?
Their flippers.

What key do whales sing in?
Sea-major.

How do fish weigh themselves?
They stand on their scales.

How do fish shop for groceries?
With a shopping carp.

Who was the most artistic fish in the sea?
Mackerel-angelo.

What are the greediest fish?
Shellfish.

Where do trout keep their money?
In the riverbank.

What is a sailor's favorite snack?
Chocolate ship cookies.

Where does a sailor go when his sail gets a hole in it?
To a whole-sail store.

What is the best day for sailing?
Winds-day.

What's a sailor's favorite food?
Naval oranges.

What happens when a sailboat gets too old?
It keels over.

Why was the Queen Mary such a good ocean liner?
It was a ship off the old dock.

What kind of truck turns into a submarine?
One with four-wheel dive.

Knock-knock.
Who's there?
Wade.
Wade who?
Wade out there and see how deep the water is, would ya?

What would you get if you crossed a fish and a tuxedo?
A swim suit.

What's the best dessert in the sea?
Octo-pie.

What did one otter say to the other when the school bell rang?
"Otter go inside now!"

How did the otter call for assistance?
"Kelp! Kelp!"

Why did the girl take her puppy to the aquarium?
She wanted to see a dogfish.

What do you call a royal seabird?
A regal seagull.

How does a cowboy cross the ocean?
On his seahorse.

What do you call a crab that gossips?
A blabby crabby.

How do you steam a clam?
Make it wait for three hours.

What is an oyster's favorite food?
Sandwiches.

What is an oyster's favorite sandwich?
Cream cheese and jellyfish.

What kind of fish does nose jobs?
A plastic sturgeon.

Why do fish that play basketball always get caught?
Because they get nothing but net.

Unwritten Books

Deep-Sea Diving by Don I. Gogh.

Whales and Other Sea Mammals by Dolly Finn.

Beachcombing Crafts by Purdy C. Shells.

After the Beach by Sandy Britches.

How did the Atlantic Ocean greet the Pacific Ocean?
It waved.

5. School Time Snickers

What's the first thing sea animals learn in school?
Their A-B-Seas.

What's a firefly's favorite part of school?
Glow and Tell.

Dorky Definitions

Antelope: When insects run away and get married.

Antifreeze: When your mom's sister gets a chill.

Appoint: The thing at the end of your pencil.

Ballroom: A nursery for crying babies.

Catalyst: What cats bring when they go food shopping.

Dorky Definitions

Debase: What a baseball player tags while running.

Debate: What you put on a fishing hook.

Deceit: What you sit on in school.

Hard drive: Six people traveling cross-country in a small car.

Kidnap: When a baby goat sleeps.

Pronoun: Being in favor of nouns.

Theorist: The part of your body that connects your hand to your arm.

What do you call the best student at the octopus school?

A goody eight-shoes.

What kind of school do carpenters attend?

Boarding school.

What kind of school do writers attend?

Grammar school.

What kind of school do fish attend?

Fin-ishing school.

Unwritten Books

Math Made Easy by Adam Up.

Inside the Principal's Office by U.R.N. Trubble.

Making New Friends by Jovanna Play.

Having a Positive Attitude by U. Ken Duitt.

Getting Good Grades by U. R. Smart.

How did the geometry teacher grade her students?
   Fair and square.

What did the chef learn at music lessons?
   How to tune a piano.

Why was the music teacher absent?
   She had minor surgery.

Tongue Twisters: Can You Say Them Five Times?

Tiny Tim tinted ten tin tents today.

She should see Shelly sell shelves.

Buddy Bidda bought a bag of Buddha bobbles.

Penny Potter ought to pack a pot of purple poppies.

We will whistle well while wearing white watches.

Why didn't the horses elect a class president?
They all voted nay.

Knock-knock.
Who's there?
Skipper.
Skipper who?
Skipper class and she'll give you detention.

PRINCIPAL: Mike, leave the door ajar when you leave.

MIKE: Okay, but give me a few minutes to find one.

What's a teacher's favorite flavor?
Chalk-olate.

TEACHER: Cindy, can you spell "rabbit"?

CINDY: "R-A-I-T."

TEACHER: What happened to the B's?

CINDY: I guess they flew away.

How does the solar system keep up its pants?
With an asteroid belt.

Knock-knock.
Who's there?
Otto.
Otto who?
Otto get going or we'll miss the bus!

Knock-knock.
Who's there?
Dewey.
Dewey who?
Dewey have a spelling test today?

Knock-knock.
Who's there?
Warner.
Warner who?
Warner about the big test on Friday!

Knock-knock.
Who's there?
Terra.
Terra who?
Terra piece of paper out of your notebook.

6. Silly Science

COUGH!

Which planet is the smoggiest?
Pollute-o.

Which planet is the most musical?
Nep-tune.

What was Cinderella's favorite constellation?
The Big Slipper.

Why did Mars and Earth collide on their trip around the sun?
They didn't planet very well.

What do you call a smart aleck space traveler?
A sasstronaut.

Why do astronauts brush after every meal?
To avoid "plaque holes."

What sport requires bats and astronauts?
Spaceball.

Why was the cow a super astronaut?
She knew all about the Milky Way.

Why were dinosaurs so sloppy?
They lived in the Mess-ozoic Era.

Which dinosaur slept alone?
Stego-snore-us.

Where did the triceratops buy its horns?
At the dino-store.

What kind of computers did dinosaurs use?
The kind with megabytes.

What goes, "Swoosh-swoosh-swoosh-thunk!"?
A blindfolded pterodactyl.

Why didn't the dinosaur understand the ptero-dactyl's jokes?

They went right over its head.

Why were tyrannosaurs always late for school?

Because it took them so long to brush all their teeth.

What was the hardest part of school for the tyrannosaur?

Final Rex-ams.

What do you call a cloning scientist?
  Gene.

How do biologists talk to each other?
  With their cell phones.

What's a geologist's favorite part of the pizza?
  The crust.

What did the geologist say after the big earthquake?
  "It's not my fault!"

What kind of cane makes people run?
  A hurry-cane.

Why did they name a hurricane Queen Victoria?
  Because she reigned for so long.

What do you call a kid who's been left out in the rain?
  Rusty.

Why was the veterinarian afraid to go out in the rain?
  She didn't want to step into a poodle.

Why was the weatherman so happy?
  Because snow news is good news.

Who tried to invent an airplane without wings?
  The Wrong Brothers.

Why did the volcano throw a fit?
It needed to blow off some steam.

RAY: Do you know where to catch your flight when you get to the airport?
KAY: Sure—it'll be plane to see.

Why do trees have roots to hold them down?
Because they're always trying to leaf.

What do you call a kid who lives in the forest?
Buck.

How did the steam engine make it up the hill?
It trained all summer.

What did the little boy say when his snowman kept melting?

"It's snow use."

SNOWMAN #1: How are you doing?
SNOWMAN #2: Snow-snow.

DAD: Why do you want to drive a snowplow?
SON: Because there's no business like snow business.

Knock-knock.
Who's there?
Vera.
Vera who?
Vera to the left so you'll miss the tree!

7. The School of Hard Knock-Knocks

Knock-Knock.
Who's there?
Anita.
Anita who?
Anita get up but I'm too sleepy.

Knock-Knock.
Who's there?
Ashby.
Ashby who?
Ashby in my fireplace.

Knock-knock.
Who's there?
Ben.
Ben who?
Ben roaming around and now I'm lost.

Knock-Knock.
Who's there?
Bennett.
Bennett who?
Bennett the vending machine again?

Knock-Knock.
Who's there?
Bingham.
Bingham who?
Bingham back some bread from the store!

Knock-knock.
Who's there?
Boris.
Boris who?
Boris with more stories and we'll leave!

Knock-knock.
  Who's there?
Carl.
  Carl who?
Carl your grandma. She misses you.

> Knock-Knock.
>   *Who's there?*
> Cassius.
>   *Cassius who?*
> Cassius good to have in the bank.

Knock-knock.
  Who's there?
Dakota.
  Dakota who?
Dakota's in da closet.

> Knock-Knock.
>   *Who's there?*
> Denise.
>   *Denise who?*
> Denise are connected to the thigh
> bones.

Knock-Knock.
  Who's there?
Distill.
  Distill who?
Distill Mary's house?

Knock-knock.
Who's there?
Doggone.
Doggone who?
Doggone for a ride in the car.

Knock-Knock.
Who's there?
Eudora.
Eudora who?
Eudora is locked. I can't get in!

Knock-knock.
Who's there?
Eugene.
Eugene who?
Eugene's have a rip in them.

Knock-knock.
>*Who's there?*

Felice.
>*Felice who?*

Felice are on my dog.

Knock-knock.
>*Who's there?*

Gladys.
>*Gladys who?*

Gladys Friday!

Knock-Knock.
>*Who's there?*

Hutch.
>*Hutch who?*

Gesundheit!

Knock-knock.
>*Who's there?*

Ida.
>*Ida who?*

Ida come over
but I got a code
in my doze.

Knock-Knock.
Who's there?
Jeanette.
Jeanette who?
Jeanette a fish?

Knock-Knock.
Who's there?
July.
July who?
July or tell the truth?

Knock-knock.
Who's there?
Ken.
Ken who?
Ken I go out and play?

Knock-knock.
Who's there?
Kenya.
Kenya who?
Kenya hear me knocking?

Knock-Knock.
Who's there?
Knox.
Knox who?
Knock-Knox on the door.

Knock-Knock.
Who's there?
Knox.
Knox who?
Knock-Knox on the door.

Knock-Knock.
Who's there?
Fred.
Fred who?
Fred I was going to say Knox again,
weren't you?

Knock-knock.
Who's there?
Lena.
Lena who?
Lena over here and give
me a hug!

Knock-knock.
Who's there?
Loman.
Loman who?
Loman on the totem pole.

Knock-knock.
Who's there?
Lotta.
Lotta who?
Lotta help you are. I had to empty
the garbage all by myself!

Knock-knock.
Who's there?
Mountain.
Mountain who?
Mountain a horse is hard.

Knock-Knock.
Who's there?
Olive.
Olive who?
Olive down the street. Want to be
friends?

Knock-knock.
Who's there?
Pasture.
Pasture who?
Pasture bedtime, isn't it?

64

Knock-knock.
  Who's there?
Randy.
  Randy who?
Randy whole way—whew! I'm out of breath!

  Knock-knock.
    Who's there?
  Rhoda.
    Rhoda who?
  Rhoda scooter all the way over here!

Knock-knock.
Who's there?
Roman.
Roman who?
Roman around the neighborhood
and thought I'd drop by.

Knock-knock.
Who's there?
Sara.
Sara who?
Sara way out of here? I'm lost!

Knock-knock.
Who's there?
Seymour.
Seymour who?
Seymour birds with these binoculars.

Knock-Knock.
Who's there?
Telly.
Telly who?
Telly phone for you!

Knock-knock.
Who's there?
Titus.
Titus who?
He Titus shoes too tight!

Knock-knock.
Who's there?
Trixie.
Trixie who?
Trixie treat and happy Halloween!

Knock-knock.
  Who's there?
Wilma.
  Wilma who?
Wilma ride be here soon?

      Knock-knock.
        Who's there?
      Woody.
        Woody who?
      Woody mind if I came in?

Knock-knock.
  Who's there?
Zeke.
  Zeke who?
Zeke ze truth and it well zet you free.

8. Holiday Ha-Ha's

How do you know when Santa Claus is in a room?
You can sense his presents.

How does a rhinoceros celebrate New Year's Eve?
By blowing its horn.

What do sheep sing on their birthdays?
"Happy Birthday to Ewe!"

Wacky Words of Affection

What did one insect say to the other?
"Bee my sweetheart!"

What did one porcupine say to the other porcupine?
"I'm stuck on you!"

What did one letter say to the other?
"You send me."

What did one acrobat say to the other acrobat?
"I'm head over heels in love with you."

What kind of flowers kiss on Valentine's Day?
  Tulips.

What do cats send on Valentine's Day?
  Love litters.

What's it called when two fish are sweet on each other?
  Guppy love.

How did the elephant and the ant start dating?
  It began as a crush.

What did the Easter bunny say about its eggs?
"They're to dye for."

What do you get when the Easter Bunny shows up
in October?
A hoppy Halloween.

What do football players carve at Halloween?
Jock-o'lanterns.

What do ducks put in their windows at Halloween?
Quack-o-lanterns.

Unwritten Books

Indoor Winter Fun by Shirley Snowden.

Christmas Treats by Candie Kane.

Sledding Disasters by C.D. Tree.

Kissing the Blarney Stone by Ken U. Pucker.

Chocolate Bunny Mishaps by Melton N.D. Sun.

Our National Anthem by Jose Canusi.

The Best Halloween Costumes by M.I. Scary.

What's big, spooky, and prevents forest fires?
Smokey the Scare.

What do ghosts wear at the beach?
Sun scream.

What do you get when you cross a cow with Frankenstein?

A moo-nster.

How do you get rid of a monster under your bed?

Give him a hang-glider and tell him to take a flying leap.

Who is the scariest fish at Halloween?

The great fright shark.

How do ghosts travel?

In fright trains.

What kind of shoes do ghosts wear?

Boo-ts.

What is a slime creature's favorite movie?

The Wizard of Ooze.

Which fairy tale is about a vampire and a monster?

Batty and the Beast.

What does a modern witch ride?

A vacuum cleaner.

What is a witch's best subject in school?

Spelling.

What did the skeleton say to the little dog?

"I've got a bone to pick with you!"

Why did the Pilgrims have a concert when they landed in America?

They wanted to see Plymouth Rock.

What did they call the friendliest people on the Mayflower?

Palgrims.

Which is correct? "A turkey's teeth are white," or "A turkey's teeth is white"?

Neither; turkeys don't have teeth.

Who visits your cat every December?
Santa Claws.

What shark visits the shore at Christmas?
Santa Jaws.

What do turtles sing at Christmas?
"Jingle shells, jingle shells..."

What do waterfowl sing at Christmas?
"Duck the Halls."

Knock-knock.
Who's there?
Yule.
Yule who?
Yule be sorry if you eat those leftovers!

What is a pop musician's favorite part of Christmas?
Rapping presents.

What did the mouse want for Christmas?
Par-cheese-ey.

What do cheese lovers sing at Christmas?
"You cheddar watch out, you cheddar not cry..."

9. **H**ilarious **H**obbies

What has letters and dashes?
A mail carrier who's running late.

What two letters describe a plant?
I.V.

What two letters describe a skating rink?
I.C.

Why is the letter "S" so powerful?
It can make a "mall" become "small."

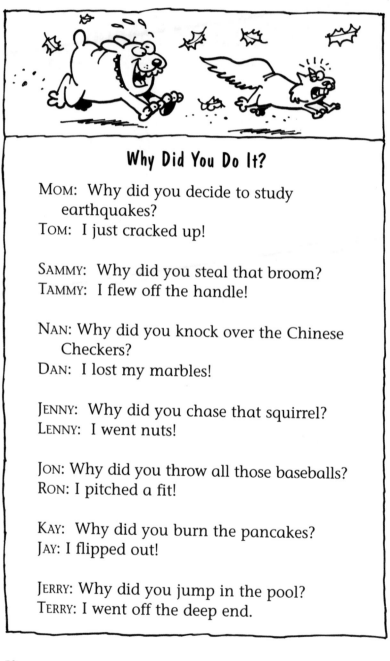

Why Did You Do It?

MOM: Why did you decide to study
earthquakes?
TOM: I just cracked up!

SAMMY: Why did you steal that broom?
TAMMY: I flew off the handle!

NAN: Why did you knock over the Chinese
Checkers?
DAN: I lost my marbles!

JENNY: Why did you chase that squirrel?
LENNY: I went nuts!

JON: Why did you throw all those baseballs?
RON: I pitched a fit!

KAY: Why did you burn the pancakes?
JAY: I flipped out!

JERRY: Why did you jump in the pool?
TERRY: I went off the deep end.

What has eight legs and spins?
Four ballerinas.

Who would you get if you crossed a ballerina and an inventor?
Leotardo DaVinci.

What do you call an artistic farm animal?
Vincent Van Goat.

Knock-Knock.
Who's there?
Disguise.
Disguise who?
Disguise the best comedian I ever heard!

What do maids like to do in their free time?
Play mop-scotch.

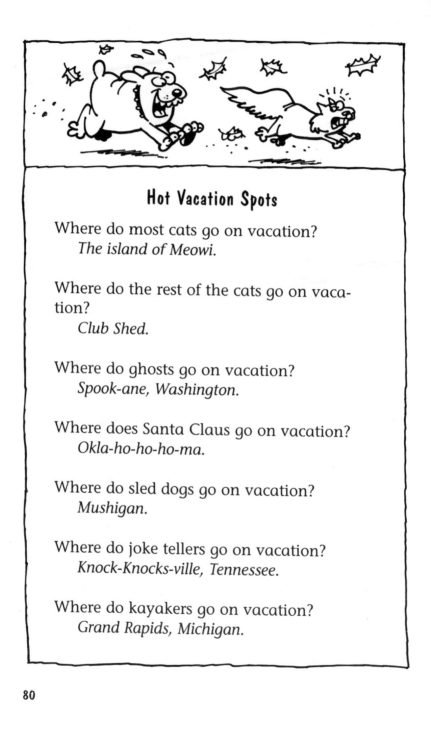

Hot Vacation Spots

Where do most cats go on vacation?
The island of Meowi.

Where do the rest of the cats go on vacation?
Club Shed.

Where do ghosts go on vacation?
Spook-ane, Washington.

Where does Santa Claus go on vacation?
Okla-ho-ho-ho-ma.

Where do sled dogs go on vacation?
Mushigan.

Where do joke tellers go on vacation?
Knock-Knocks-ville, Tennessee.

Where do kayakers go on vacation?
Grand Rapids, Michigan.

Why couldn't the dancer finish the competition?
He was all tapped out.

What's the best city for wandering around?
Rome.

Why did the man put a stamp on his forehead?
He thought he was a first-class male.

Did you read the book about the dieting cow?
It's called Skinnie the Moo.

What did the lamp say to Aladdin?
"You rub me the wrong way!"

Performances to Remember

Why was the garbage collector booed off the stage?

His act stank.

Why was the cheese shredder cheered on stage?

His act was grate.

Why was the kangaroo given a standing ovation?

Its talents were boundless.

Why did the ice sculptor win an award?

His statues were cool!

Why was the cow such a good comedian?

It was udderly ridiculous!

Wouldn't It Be Hilarious If...

A furniture builder lost his drawers.

A pastry chef was half-baked.

A detective was clueless.

An egg farmer cracked up.

An auto mechanic was exhausted.

An artist gave you the brush-off.

A cashew grower went nuts.

An underwear salesperson was brief.

A gardener was bushed.

A chef was a crackpot.

Wouldn't It Be Hilarious If...

A nurse called all the shots.

A plumber was a real drip.

A photographer didn't get the big picture.

A veterinarian went to the dogs.

A carpenter had a screw loose.

A film developer had a negative attitude.

An acupuncturist felt pointless.

A fisherman was crabby.

A door hanger became unhinged.

A rapper was all tied up.

What would you get if you crossed a bird and a tuxedo?

A penguin.

What do you call an artistic cow?

Rembranded.

What do you call painting classes for sheriffs?

Marshall arts.

Did you hear about the new movie about a duck that lays golden eggs?

It's called Quack and the Beanstalk.

What movie would Pinocchio star in if he were royalty?

The Lyin' King.

Tongue Twisters: Can You Say Them Five Times?

Tethered leather weathers well in better weather.

Three thick thieves see thirty-three safes.

Why did the man use a baseball bat to do yard work?

He was beating around the bush.

Did you hear about the new computer bug? One byte and you're a goner!

LEE: I went camping and now I itch all over from biting flies.

VEE: Maybe you shouldn't have bitten so many of them!

10. Grab Bag Gags

Knock-knock.
Who's there?
Wilder.
Wilder who?
Wilder beasts live in Africa.

What does Tarzan say about swinging through the jungle?
"It's de-vine!"

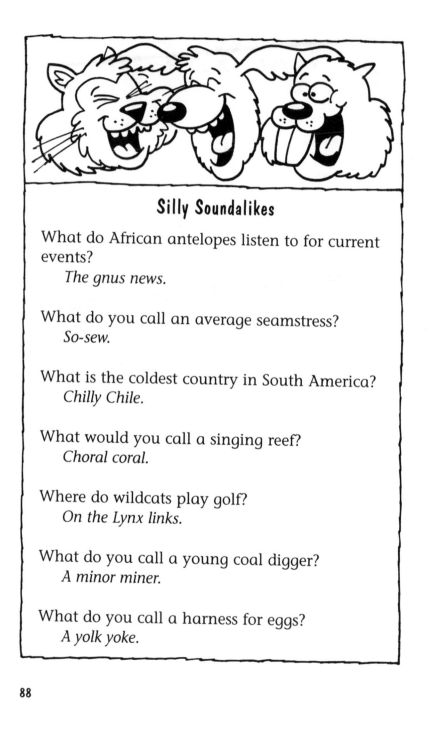

Silly Soundalikes

What do African antelopes listen to for current events?
The gnus news.

What do you call an average seamstress?
So-sew.

What is the coldest country in South America?
Chilly Chile.

What would you call a singing reef?
Choral coral.

Where do wildcats play golf?
On the Lynx links.

What do you call a young coal digger?
A minor miner.

What do you call a harness for eggs?
A yolk yoke.

What parties do bushes give for their dolls?
Tree-parties.

Why was the tree released from prison?
It decided to turn over a new leaf.

What doesn't have a body, but has two legs and runs?
A pair of pantyhose.

How do girl pigs wear their hair?
In people-tails.

How do horses wear their hair?
In ponytails.

What do a cat, an author, and a kite have in common?

They all have tails.

What do a kangaroo, a dress, and a parachutist have in common?

They're all jumpers.

What do a mother deer, a baker, and a banker have in common?

They all have a little doe.

Did you hear about the girl who bought perfume from a skunk?

She fell for it...hook, line and stinker.

Why did the girl put bandages on her bedroom window?

She was told the window had pains.

Why did the boy have feathers on his shoes?

He was pigeon-toed.

Why did this author get to create this book?

Because she had the write stuff.

What do you call a girl who gets up early?

Dawn.

When are most twins born?

On Twos-day.

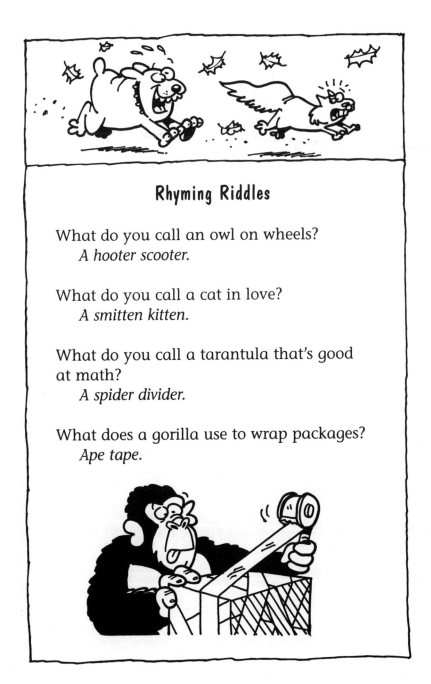

Rhyming Riddles

What do you call an owl on wheels?
A hooter scooter.

What do you call a cat in love?
A smitten kitten.

What do you call a tarantula that's good at math?
A spider divider.

What does a gorilla use to wrap packages?
Ape tape.

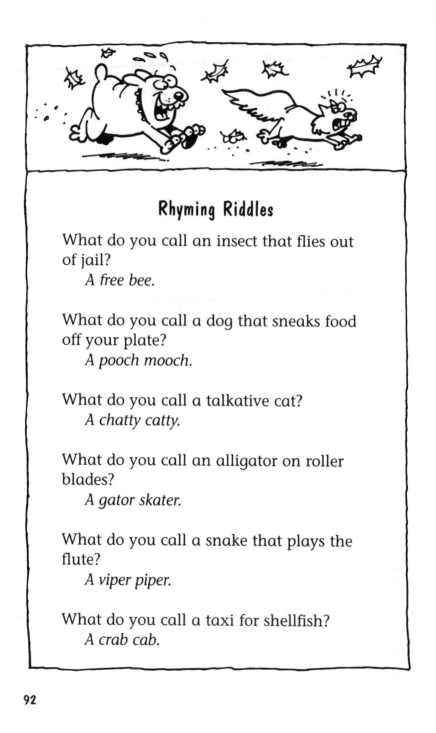

Rhyming Riddles

What do you call an insect that flies out of jail?

A free bee.

What do you call a dog that sneaks food off your plate?

A pooch mooch.

What do you call a talkative cat?

A chatty catty.

What do you call an alligator on roller blades?

A gator skater.

What do you call a snake that plays the flute?

A viper piper.

What do you call a taxi for shellfish?

A crab cab.

Rhyming Riddles

What do you call a fat cat?
A flabby tabby.

What does a tortoise leap over for fun?
A turtle hurdle.

What vehicle do you use to rescue a
kangaroo?
A hopper chopper.

What do you call a flying insect that's
running out of gas?
A sputter-by butterfly.

What do you call a rodent with rhythm?
A rat-a-tat-tat.

What do you call a pick-up full of
chickens?
A cluck truck.

What can you always leave behind and never need to get back?

Your footprints.

Why did Peg Leg the Pirate lose control over his crew?

He couldn't put his foot down.

Knock-knock.

Who's there?

Polygon.

Polygon who?

Polygon bye-bye!

Index